XII

THE code

It's time for a new kind of man

Carl Beech,
Andy Drake
& Ian Manifold

MONARCH
BOOKS
Oxford, UK & Grand Rapids, Michigan, USA

First published in the UK in 2011 by Monarch Books (a publishing imprint of Lion Hudson plc)
Wilkinson House, Jordan Hill Road, Oxford OX2 8DR, England
Tel: +44 (0)1865 302750 Fax: +44 (0)1865 302757
Email: monarch@lionhudson.com
www.lionhudson.com

ISBN 978 0 85721 022 7 (print)
ISBN 978 0 85721 131 6 (epub)
ISBN 978 0 85721 130 9 (Kindle)
ISBN 978 0 85721 132 3 (PDF)

Distributed by:
UK: Marston Book Services, PO Box 269, Abingdon, Oxon, OX14 4YN
USA: Kregel Publications, PO Box 2607, Grand Rapids, Michigan 49501

MIX
Paper from responsible sources
FSC® C022612
www.fsc.org

The text paper used in this book has been made from wood independently certified as having come from sustainable forests.

British Library Cataloguing Data
A catalogue record for this book is available from the British Library.

Printed and bound in Malta by Gutenberg Press.

The Code

JESUS IS MY CAPTAIN, BROTHER, RESCUER AND FRIEND.

I OWE EVERYTHING TO HIM. I WILL DO ANYTHING FOR HIM.

I WILL UNASHAMEDLY MAKE HIM KNOWN THROUGH MY ACTIONS AND WORDS.

I WILL NOT CHEAT IN ANYTHING, PERSONAL OR PROFESSIONAL.

I WILL LOOK AWAY FROM THE GUTTER, BUT BE PREPARED TO PULL PEOPLE OUT OF IT.

I WILL KEEP MY BODY FIT AND FREE FROM ANY ADDICTIONS.

I WILL PUT THE WELFARE OF THOSE CLOSEST TO ME BEFORE MY OWN WELFARE.

I WILL TREAT ALL MEN AND WOMEN AS BROTHERS AND SISTERS.

I WILL LEAD AS HE WOULD LEAD. I WILL HONOUR MY LEADERS PROVIDED THIS ALSO HONOURS HIM. I WILL FOLLOW HIM IN COMPANY WITH MY SISTERS AND BROTHERS.

I WILL USE MY STRENGTH TO PROTECT THE WEAK AND STAND AGAINST THE ABUSE OF POWER.

I WILL PROTECT THE WORLD THAT GOD HAS MADE.

IF I FAIL I WILL NOT GIVE UP. HE NEVER GIVES UP ON ME.

CONTENTS

ACKNOWLEDGMENTS

Carl Beech
Life changed for me at the age of 18 when I met Jesus. This manual is ultimately for Him and His fame and glory. To anyone reading this or dipping into it who doesn't know Him, I say check Him and His teaching out. It will blow you away. If you know Him and are struggling, I hope this gives you strength and help. Don't quit: keep plugging away. So, a simple word of thanks to all those who have had a hand in this, namely my mates, mentors, family, and the band of brothers that is Christian Vision for Men (CVM) and Codelife. Special mentions go to Karen (for being an awesome wife and proofreader), Emily and Annie, the CVM team of Joe M, Jonathan S, Dave L, Alex W, and the band of brothers across the UK. Also to Andy D, Ian M, John Glass, Lyndon Bowring, Graham Kendrick, Lee and Baz, Roy Crowne, Eric Delve, the team at Monarch for grabbing hold of this, the Cape Town conspirators (you know who you are and I know you value your anonymity), and all those I have offended by accidentally missing your names out!

Ian Manifold
My thanks go to Carl for having the vision for the Code – and to God for, as we humbly

trust, giving it to him. My thanks go to both Carl and Andy for the pleasure I've had and the graciousness they've shown to me and to each other as I've worked with them on this project. I thank those who have given me advice on specialist areas and references and I especially thank my wife Gillian for her support for my involvement in this work. One great encouragement has been that although I find following Jesus difficult, and at times I still wrestle with questions which aren't finally answered and with lingering frustrations, this project reinforced for me again that trusting in the life and death and resurrection and message of Jesus and trying to follow Him is the best answer I've yet found to life and death and to what this world throws at me.

Andy Drake

Thanks to my great friends (you know who you are!) who have challenged and guided me over the years, and who have also demonstrated that godliness and fun are not diametrically opposed! I look forward to finishing well with you all and then partying for ever.

FOREWORD

The Code is a fantastic manual for practical Christian living. Reading it could radically change your life! Carl Beech is a "man after God's own heart", a 21st century young David who's seeing giants slain in the lives of men. I believe the ministry to men God is raising up under Carl's leadership is one of the most exciting moves I have witnessed in recent years. The more we equip men to live in a godly way, the greater their impact at home, at work, in the local church and in the wider community. Carl is inspiring men to do just this.

It's a privilege to know him, work with him, pray for him – and love him deeply.

Lyndon Bowring
Executive Chairman, CARE

PREFACE

The average man has just shy of 80 years
to leave his mark. And I want to live my life
well. I want to rinse life of every opportunity
to make a real difference, leaving a lasting
legacy for the King and His Kingdom.

But a battle is raging. A battle within, with the
pungent realities of lust, greed and pride... a
battle with the world with its heady cocktail
of temptation and distorted definition of
success... and ultimately, a battle with the
powers of evil that threaten to drain hope and
choke life.

And that is why I have signed up to Codelife.
With a bold vision of what can be and a wary
understanding of the realities that threaten
that potential, Codelife is a standard that will
help me navigate the choices I make every
day. For me, Codelife is a solid reminder that
knowing Jesus comes first and everything
else flows out of that... Let's get living it!

Andy Frost
Director, Share Jesus International

INTRODUCTION

Physically, this is a small book. However, it comes to you after a long journey that began over twenty years ago.

There are a few men out there who know me really well. In fact, they know me warts and all. These are the blokes I really laugh, cry, wrestle (verbally and sometimes physically), and row with. I'm not sure what they would say if you were to ask them what I am really like, but I do know they see me as very far from perfect. I get quite a lot wrong, quite a lot of the time. I am, however, passionate about Jesus and seeing the Kingdom of God at work.

The day I met Jesus (on 22 April 1990 at about 7 p.m.) was simultaneously shattering, devastating, life changing, exhilarating, heartbreaking, and totally awe-inspiring. Forty-five minutes later I got up to leave the little chapel where I had just met Him. Standing on the steps outside, I had tears streaming down my face as I looked at a half-dead small tree on the other side of the road. It was as if I had never seen leaves on trees before. The colours just hit me. I remember driving home, looking at people and feeling overwhelmed with emotion.

"These are people that God has made... and He loves them..."

I knew then that I would dedicate all of my energy and efforts to making Jesus known to people. I distinctly heard God call me to "fight a different sort of battle" – which resulted in my immediately giving up a boyhood dream of joining the armed forces. This wasn't because of any moral conviction about fighting: I just knew that God was calling me to something very different.

And so the adventure began – and at times it's been really tough.

My life of faith has been punctuated by significant ups and downs. I find it hard to be the man I know I ought to be. I find it hard to keep my life pure. I find that passion ebbs and flows as I deal with disappointments, opposition, and apathy in others and myself. The rogue in me often rises to the surface, and I haven't always made my frustration my friend in a way that empowers and brings life. All too often I've let frustration eat at me rather than using it to compel me to action.

I can, however, honestly say that since that day in April 1990 I've wanted to be a man of devotion and prayer as well as action. I've wanted and pursued a deeply close walk with my brother, captain, and friend, Jesus, but I have fallen short so many times. Like many men I've felt guilty over missed, snatched, or hurried times of prayer and reading the Bible. Like many men I've struggled silently in church settings (even when I was a leader), and like many men I have gone through long periods of feeling like a fraud. You need to know that I'm not what you might think I am. I am a weird mix of things, from loving playing the piano and writing poems to shooting things and burning stuff and doing mad endurance challenges! I like nothing more than laughing with mates and chilling out with my girls (wife and daughters). I'm competitive, can lose my rag, can be a bit intense and at times noisy and chaotic. Within all that, I follow Jesus with a passion. It's just that working out what it is to be a man and a Jesus-follower can sometimes be tricky.

But several things have kept me going through the ups and downs:

1. I prayed to Jesus, the day I met Him, that I would go wherever He asked me to go and do whatever He wanted me to do... no matter what. I try to be a man of my word, and I think in turn God loves that kind of prayer and has intercepted me at times when I have been wavering.

2. My mates who journey with me have picked me up when I needed it.

3. Jesus loves me.

4. I believe completely in the power and reality of the gospel and in the fact that the only way to God is through Jesus. How can I stay silent?

5. God has given me a vision for reaching men.

But still I struggled... And then, after a number of years in financial sales, and time spent first as a church planter on a tough estate and then as a senior pastor, I found myself as part of a men's ministry team.

I joined Christian Vision for Men (CVM) from being the senior leader of a large church. It was a period of time which gave me much to thank God for. I had far too much ego, pride, and self-belief, and God, in His wisdom, knew I needed it knocked out of me. So for two years I was no longer "the leader" and spent my time passionately seeking to serve another man's vision.

Some men have subsequently told me that they could never lay down senior leadership to work under someone again. In my opinion, these men should not be in leadership. Serving another man and his vision was a special time that contributed hugely to what follows.

About three years ago, just after I started to lead CVM, I was standing in the shower when I felt God speak to me with a clarity and certainty that I have rarely encountered. I was actually praying at the time, asking God for the key that would see at least 1 million men in the UK come to faith. And then it happened. I had what I can only describe as a "download" moment.

Stepping out of the shower, I dried off and immediately wrote down on a scrap of paper: "THE CODE".

This was followed by four hurriedly written statements, which I had barely begun to think through.

I had the vision but not the detail.

The vision that swept through my heart and mind was of a viral, mass movement of men based around a kind of new faith order, a Jesus-centred rule of life.

I took the vision and the rough details to my team and got the following response: "This is of God... but the statements you have written are from you; and to be honest, mate, they're not very good!"

Humbling, or what?

And so began a two-year journey of trying to unpack the Code and write something that would be a catalyst, helping men to come to faith through the actions of believing men who were empowered, fired up, and full of faith.

We wanted to write something that would cover the essential elements of words and actions when it came to communicating the gospel. We wanted to look at critical areas in life, from leadership to tackling injustice. What you have here is the end product. It's birthed out of years of debate, conversation, and a fair amount of passion to see the kingdom come. I hope you are engaged by what God has given us. And so the Codelife movement has begun. As I write this in Cape Town, we are hearing requests from men who want to launch the movement in South Africa, Canada, and Europe. We didn't expect that!

Sometimes people ask me what it means to actually join the movement. Well, read on. But be assured: this is a movement for men who want to make their lives count, even if it means one day laying them down. It is a movement of men who are unashamed of the cross and who are deeply committed to doing whatever it takes to be a man of the Kingdom. It is also a movement of men who know that they are likely to mess things up. Passionate, full-on men tend to mess things up quite a lot! So if that sounds like you... read on. If you wish you were like that but aren't quite sure... read on.

To all those men out there who have joined
this movement, I salute your courage and
welcome you to this amazing brotherhood.
Welcome to the movement of the unashamed.
May boldness be our friend and Jesus our
commander.

Carl Beech

INTRODUCING IAN AND ANDY

Ian and Andy are "the brothers" whom I invited to help me because they have the same conviction and heart to see a movement of men stirred up. They are the co-founders of this movement.

Andy was born and bred in Australia and has variously been a dustman, labourer, IT man, and church leader. He loves good food, fast cars, the beach, and sport (particularly football and skiing). He has helped to lead three churches over the last fifteen years and is married to Sophie, a clinical psychologist. Andy and I have known each other for many years and have contended for the gospel through thick and thin. We can wind each other up, tell each other as it is, laugh till we feel sick, and totally trust each other. We've got each other's backs, and that's priceless.

Ian hails from Sheffield and is also one of my greatest mates. He is a cancer specialist, and also does work for the government which I don't really understand but means that he has a huge brain! He is one of the fittest men I know (he would add, "for my age") and has cycled with me across the UK, France, and Italy. He used to be a mountaineer, until a "touching the void" experience made him hang up his crampons. Ian is also one of those men who out of his love and concern for you will say the difficult thing. Again, it's a priceless friendship. Ian is married to Gill and has two grown-up daughters.

These two "brothers" are the ones who wrestled with, prayed for, and shaped the twelve principles that follow. Truth be known, the three of us have got some battle scars and campaign medals from following the way of Jesus. We've hung on in there and desire nothing more than to finish strong and take some mates with us. That's what Codelife is all about.

How do I use *The Code*?

What you are looking at now is the manual of the Codelife movement. Inside this "back pocket" book you will find short chapters on each point of the Code, with prayers and even a poem. Basically, you can read it through in one go, dip in and out as you want to, and use it to help your own private time with God or even as material for a group discussion. It's up to you! You will find it a flexible resource to help you walk closely with Jesus, perhaps over many years. Tied in with this book is a whole heap of resources on the internet at www.codelife.org. There you will find a year's worth of Bible studies, multimedia material, testimonies, and much more.

You will have to work out for yourself what each part of the Code means to you. We hope that this is a journey that you go on with a few mates and that as a result we will see many men around the world challenged to follow Jesus – more accurately, to live lives full-on for Jesus.

How do I join the movement?

That's the easy bit. We would simply say that you need to think it through carefully and pray about it. Perhaps you might want to pledge to live by the Code with other men in your church. At the end of this book is an expanded version of the Code that you might want to use as a statement or prayer of personal commitment.

Having decided to take that step, some guys have used fasting as an entry point. Others simply meet together to pray, share life, and commit to support one another to live by the Code's promises, perhaps using the prayers at the back.

Each year we run camps and conferences where we pledge, in some cases around the world's biggest bonfire, to continue to live by the Code.

Then comes the tough bit. Beside each point of the Code, at the back of this manual, you have the chance to write down what living by the Code will mean to you: in other words, what action will you take?

Oh, and just one more thing. If you want to get emails and resources and let us know about the step you have taken, you simply sign up at www.codelife.org.

So, in bullet points, you join by:

- thinking and praying hard about this lifetime commitment to a biblical rule of life.

- praying and fasting (if you can).

- covenanting to live by the Code (preferably with others).

- forming a small group and committing to turn up.

- reading through the manual and starting to use the resources on www.codelife.org.

- taking action with others based around the Code (see appendix, where you can write this for yourself).

- attending an annual Codelife camp as a way of restating your commitment.

- praying daily for your brothers in the movement.

- praying daily for those you know who don't know Jesus.

- seeking to introduce other men to Codelife.

1

JESUS IS MY CAPTAIN, BROTHER, RESCUER, AND FRIEND

(CARL)

They say that in the heat of battle, "Chesty" Puller, who retired from the US Marines as a lieutenant general, would bark out orders in a voice that could rattle the gates of hell, and that he would stalk about with his chest puffed out, despite the incoming enemy fire, as if he were daring anyone to hit him. I guess, if you've seen the movie, he was a bit like the colonel in *Apocalypse Now* who unflinchingly and ultra-coolly strolls around a beach that's being hit by artillery shells and machine gun fire, while everyone else is diving for cover.

Chesty was, and is, a legend in the Marine Corps. It is said that even after his retirement in 1955, young marines would view it as a pilgrimage to visit his home and spend time with him and his wife. Never being a man to refuse a fight, he even tried to re-enlist at the age of 67 because he didn't want to miss out on a fight in Vietnam! He was refused.

He had seen action in so many conflicts that he was awarded a total of five Navy Crosses. No other US marine has ever been so highly decorated. There is no doubt of his standing and status. Do a Google search of his name and you will have no shortage of hero-worship material to read, and some of it is cracking stuff. As a leader of men he was a class act, and there is no doubting his talent and skill. Some men just have the way of inspiring loyalty, even to death, and Chesty Puller had it in bucketloads. Just looking at an old picture online conveys the sheer charisma of the man. It's been recorded that one of his marines once said, "I'd follow that man to hell" – but he went on to say in the same sentence "and it looks as though I may have to."

As is so often the case with great men, there was a flip side to the hard-drinking, hard-fighting warrior. War to Chesty Puller was a matter of kill or be killed. He reportedly condoned the shooting of prisoners and once ordered his artillery to fire on a supporting and friendly army unit if it exposed his marines by retreating. Puller's tactics were built around one word: attack. One famous Chesty quote, from a time when he was massively outgunned and surrounded on all sides, goes something like this: "They're to the left of us, behind us, to the right of us, and in front of us. That simplifies things: they can't get away this time."

I've got to admit it, I love that kind of gung-ho stuff: it's fantastic. Reading about his life makes me want to charge alongside him in battle as well! But then you pause to think about the flip side.

What if I were the man having to follow the colonel's command to charge a well-equipped and numerically superior army? What if my life were just seen as a statistic to achieve an aim? I mean, in just one of Chesty Puller's battles, at Guadalcanal, 25,000 experienced soldiers were killed. Not so wonderful any more, is it?

So what's this got to do with following Jesus?

Well, right at the start of this manual we need to lay down some solid principles. To be a part of Codelife is to recognize that we have a leader who *doesn't* have a "flip side". He doesn't want to use you just to achieve an aim. And while following Jesus is a full-on promise, the relationship will last for eternity, not just until the fighting is over.

Firstly, as men who live by the Code we are in no doubt that Jesus is our Captain. By this we mean that we have determined to follow Him anywhere and do whatever He asks us to do. He is King Jesus, and it is a fact that He will one day judge the living and the dead (Matthew 25:31–33). In the meantime we have some standing orders in Matthew 28 to "go into the world" and some lifestyle "requests" as seen through the Gospels, particularly in Matthew 5. That means that as Jesus' soldiers, we have determined to get on with it and not to moan, sulk, or complain. We have given away our rights. We are slaves to Christ. Just as the Roman centurion in Matthew 8 recognized Jesus' authority from the perspective of a hardbitten soldier, so do we as men of God recognize that we are His to command. Our lives are not our own.

Tip number one: If there is something you are still doing that you know deep down you need to stop doing but are making excuses, reaffirm that Jesus is your Captain and submit to His lead.

Secondly, Jesus is also our brother, as seen in Mark 3:35 ("Whoever does God's will is my brother and sister and mother"). Jesus even calls us His friends, in John 15:15. This is crucial for us men to get hold of. We have a Captain and Leader who also longs for relationship. He wants to walk with you, share life with you, get to know you. He will never leave you. We are family! In response, we need to learn to be increasingly honest in our dealings with God and work at spending quality time with Him.

Tip number two: How about building in some regular "relationship time" to your life? It may be when you are in the gym, walking the dog, or during your commute. Just do whatever works for you, but make sure you spend time with our Brother and Friend on a very regular basis. Your life will change as a result. You may not notice the difference at first, but within months you certainly will.

Thirdly, it is Jesus who has rescued us. To this day I cannot read the account of the crucifixion without something of a lump in my throat. As men we must never allow ourselves to make our faith merely an academic exercise. It has to be a heart thing as well. Talk to a bloke who had his life spared by the actions of another man and you will be left in no doubt as to the overwhelming gratitude on behalf of the rescued to the rescuer. That's why Zacchaeus wanted to make up for the wrong he'd done, and why the woman washed Jesus' feet with her tears. It's the same for us guys who are part of the Codelife movement. We are literally eternally grateful. Just don't lose that sense of wonder and awe, and fight hard to keep it. This movement is characterized by men whose lives flow with grace because of the grace we know. This is a movement of men who have optimism, hope, and a sense of heaven on our shoulders. We are not moaners, sulkers, or cynics, because we know what we have been saved from.

Tip number three: Never forget your first love. Don't take yourself too seriously, but take what God is doing in and through your life very seriously.

As I reflect on this, one interesting thought springs to mind. The more I have walked in these truths, the happier I have become. In fact, I have laughed more in the last year or two than ever before. Interesting, that...

Prayer

Father, I state now before You that Jesus is my Captain, Brother, Rescuer, and Friend. He is my leader, and Your word is my final authority in all things. I will not be ashamed of Him and I will never disavow Him. Help me never to walk away and always to walk closely with Him on the narrow path. Amen.

"I am the way and the truth and the life."

JESUS CHRIST OF NAZARETH

2

I OWE EVERYTHING TO HIM. I WILL DO ANYTHING FOR HIM
(ANDY)

Owe. Everything. Anything.

Pretty powerful words.

Put together, they're not to be used lightly.
In fact, these are "once in a lifetime" words.
I might owe you money, a beer, or a favour
at work, but you're still not going to get *just
anything* from me.

To owe everything and be prepared to do
anything means something really major has
happened. Take the 1991 film *Robin Hood:
Prince of Thieves*. Azeem (played by Morgan
Freeman) swears a life debt to Robin (Kevin
Costner), after Robin saves him from a death
sentence during the Crusades. Of course, by
the end of the film he has repaid the debt by
saving Robin's life in return.

However, what we're talking about here
is a debt so massive that it can never be

repaid. Imagine, for instance, that you were responsible for deliberately releasing a deadly plague into the world and everyone became contaminated by it. Death was certain and life was now inescapably painful for all. Unless you were utterly heartless, you'd feel a little guilty. If it were me, I know I'd have enough guilt to last me a lifetime; in fact, I probably wouldn't want to live at all. But imagine God seeing you do that, and then being prepared to forgive you. You'd want to know what the catch was, and he'd say, "Simple – what you did was terrible, but I've arranged for someone else to suffer the punishment for your crime. As long as you're happy to accept that arrangement, you're free."

Again, if that were me I'd think, "This is great, but also completely unfair on whoever has been punished in my place, and I don't deserve such forgiveness anyway. It can't be true, and it shouldn't be true, because it's just not fair."

But it is true.

God's outrageous grace is needed to deal with our terrible guilt. The "deadly disease" scenario above is actually real. The man who released the deadly disease was Adam, and the subsequent sin has infected us all. But we, just like Adam, are not just the infected: *we are also the perpetrators, for we have rebelled against God and brought pain into the world.*

Just as a digital camera can stamp photos with the time and place they were taken, so our sin is real-world stuff. Every careless word, every selfish action – every lack of acknowledgment of God as God – has a moment and place in time. God sees this so clearly. If we knew just how transparent our sin was, we'd cower in shame.

Confronted with a holy God who demands that everything in His creation reflect His goodness, we have no defence; we are caught bang to rights. God is holy and therefore perfectly just, and so we must answer for every little thing.

But here is the wonder. Yes, God's holiness leads to justice. However, His love leads to mercy through outrageous forgiveness.

On the cross of Jesus, God's justice and mercy meet, and our guilt and shame are completely, 100 per cent, dealt with. It isn't fair and it isn't deserved. You and I aren't anything special in and of ourselves to warrant such an act. To even begin to suggest that we can somehow earn this forgiveness is to completely misunderstand just what was involved at Calvary. We deserve hell, but through Jesus we get heaven.

Even more amazingly, heaven starts now!
We receive the Holy Spirit so that we can
meet with God and serve Him with power;
we become changed over time so that sin no
longer rules our everyday lives; we are given
a family of like-minded people to walk with
through life, and we have a hope for eternity,
the abundance of which sometimes even
breaks through into this life.

How awesome.

You'd think that because of all this the
average Christian would be a fireball of
enthusiasm, but we know that's often not the
case. I've met so many Christians who for
one reason or another just want God to fit
into their lives, and they don't even see the
audacity of such an attitude.

There is only one response to what Jesus has
done, and that is for us to fit in with *His* plans,
and to completely and unreservedly recognize
that we belong to Him. The apostle Paul puts
it like this: we have been "bought at a price"
(1 Corinthians 6:20) and so should honour God
with our whole life.

Great men have gone before us, having lived
true to this ideal. On 3 February 1943 the
SS *Dorchester* was torpedoed at night by a
German U-boat. As the ship was sinking, a
young soldier ran up to one of the chaplains

and cried, "I've lost my life jacket." "Take this," replied the chaplain, and calmly he handed the soldier his life jacket. Before the ship sank, each chaplain gave his life jacket to another man. As the *Dorchester* went down, the chaplains linked arms and lifted their voices in prayer. You see, they knew what God had done for them, they knew what they were about, and they knew where they were going.

Doing *anything* because we owe *everything* means living with the same outrageous grace God has demonstrated to us through Jesus. Instead of just wanting to make money, carve out a career, and buy a comfy semi-detached house, we need to be asking, "God, how would you like me to be a part of the answer in this world as opposed to a part of the problem?" And when He replies, we need to step up to the plate.

Life is short – crazily so. We have one chance to "shine like the stars" so let's do anything He asks, because we owe everything to Him. It's not like we can ever pay him back, and, thank God, He's not even asking us to. We're just called to live as if God is everything. Because He is.

Prayer

All I have, and all I ever will have, is Yours. Help me to walk with a sense of heaven on my shoulders and to live accordingly. I commit to be a man of hope who knows that he has been saved by grace. Amen.

I owe everything to Him. I will do anything for Him

"Faith is a living, daring confidence in God's grace, so sure and certain that a man could stake his life on it a thousand times."

3

I WILL UNASHAMEDLY MAKE HIM KNOWN IN ALL I DO AND SAY

(IAN)

It's scary and it's depressing. They're so sure of themselves. They don't even bother to argue the toss any more, because everybody *knows* it's naff. They say, "At best it's a joke. It's worth zilch. It's just for grandmas." Or worse, "It's somewhere between mad, sad, and bad, riddled with sad weirdos who can't cope – kiddie fiddlers, women who look like men, and men who wear frocks for a uniform, ponces who like the sound of their own voice, narrow-minded, two-faced prats who say they're right and you're wrong, but they're no different than you."

They're talking about "Christianity" or "the church" or "religion". Somebody says, "It's about a bloke (one of that famous handful who started a major religion) who's supposed to have died for my 'sins'. Why? And what's 'sin' – something about living with your girlfriend without being married? So? That's normal –

so what? And He comes back from the dead (like you do), but we can't see Him – well, that's convenient! Come on! Get real!"

As I listen, I feel my defences weaken. I feel a growing sympathy with their views. I think, yeah, I see why you feel like that. My determination to speak out starts to retreat in front of an oncoming tidal wave of anxiety and hopelessness, a deadening, depressing weight. It's like a voice, inside. "What's the point of opening your mouth? It's useless. They'll either rubbish it, or ignore it. They're too set in their views, too strong – for crying out loud, they've half convinced *you*!"

Where's this deadening feeling coming from, apart from my own cowardice? It's for this very moment that I need to carry the answers inside me, learnt, ready to come instantly to the front of my mind:

- "For our struggle is not against flesh and blood, but against the rulers, against the authorities, against the powers of this dark world and against the spiritual forces of evil in the heavenly realms" (Ephesians 6:12).

- "...the one who is in you is stronger than the one who is in the world" (1 John 4:4).

- "For when I am weak, then I am strong" (2 Corinthians 12:10).

- "I am not ashamed of the gospel, because

it is the power of God for the salvation of everyone who believes" (Romans 1:16).

Also, at times like that, I should remember one morning not long ago when I stood watching a weird-looking, shiny brass bucket being swung to and fro, shedding a quiet stream of ash onto the lawn of a crematorium. Grey covered green. Death covered life. These ashes had been my father. I stood next to my mother at the crematorium. She was saying through her tears, "Scatter them over there, by the flower bed, or we'll forget where."

A few weeks before, I'd spent days by my father's deathbed as he fought grimly for breath. Then I'd watched the last breath leave his body. It had come at the end of years of deafness, blindness, pain, and increasing helplessness, made worse by a mind completely alert as he lost all his dignity, bit by relentless bit.

But forty years before that, I had sat with him and explained the gospel and, struggling with the awkwardness and embarrassment of a teenager teaching his father, I had rather reluctantly studied the Bible with him. I was there when he first decided to follow Jesus, and began a life of faith which grew stronger over a lifetime of service. It ended with him singing hymns to his carers through his suffering, and saying on his deathbed that he wasn't afraid, because he was trusting God.

I was there at his birth into a new life, and I was there at the end when he left for the next part of the journey. I was allowed to play a part in all that. What a privilege.

It boils down to this, in the end. There's life, and work, and family, and retirement, and suffering, and loss of dignity, and following Jesus, and meaning, and hope both for this life and beyond. Or there's life, and work, and family, and retirement, and suffering, and loss of dignity, and then it's, "Over there, by the flower beds, or we'll forget where." And that's it. That's it! Or something worse.

I was allowed to stand at the junction between those two ways, for my father, and help direct him. How can you put a value on that? Priceless. What about that for job satisfaction? Unbeatable. All I can do is thank God.

I'm not a minister or any form of "professional", full-time, paid Christian worker. I'm "just a punter". I struggle with everything. I find the ideas of judgment and hell appalling, but know that any view which ignores them has more problems than one which takes them into account.

I'm troubled by the problem of the people who've never heard or understood about Jesus, but I'll have to leave that to the God who loves them. I struggle with people's suffering, and as a lifelong cancer specialist, I've seen more than most. But suffering without hope and God in the world is worse than suffering with Him.

There have been times when for long periods, my mouth has been shut when it came to speaking about Jesus. I look back now and think, you fool! What a waste of time that was. But over the years, there have been a number, all too small, of people who I believe I have, with God's kindness, helped to direct to Him. I hope one day that I will find out there were many more for whom I was a "link in the chain". But I don't want to be satisfied just being an unknowing link. It's so much better *knowing* you have been used to help somebody find Him.

In recent years, by far the most encouraging aspect of my Christian life has been leaving the comfort zone of closed-in church life, crossing cultural and class barriers to share my life and my trust in the cross of Jesus with non-believing friends, and seeing them draw ever closer to becoming His followers.

So, to hell with fear and embarrassment – that's where they came from and that's where they can go. Whose reputation am I worried about? I haven't got one without Him. *His* reputation is the only one that matters. So, failing and asking for forgiveness, repaying insult and apathy with love and determination, whispering or shouting, loving it or loathing it, confident or doubting, praying all the time, through family and financial problems, illness and bereavement, let's unashamedly make Him known in all we do and say.

And when people ask why we're different (and they will), let's not keep silent in false modesty, which is an excuse for cowardice. Let's *say* that if there is anything worthwhile that they see in us, then we owe it all to the One we follow, and explain why.

When we see non-believing people through Jesus' eyes, they're not the self-assured towers of strength which we find so daunting. They think they're rich and strong, but in His eyes they're poor, weak, and naked. They need our love and friendship, not our fear and avoidance.

God says, "How beautiful on the mountains are the feet of those who bring good news" (Isaiah 52:7). Let's get ourselves a foot makeover ASAP!

Prayer

I commit to speak out at the right times and not stay silent. I will not make shallow excuses in order to get away with keeping my mouth shut. Please create for me regular opportunities to share the news about Jesus, and help me to have the right words to say at those times. In Jesus' name. Amen.

I will unashamedly make Him known in all I do and say

"We talk of the Second Coming; half the world has never heard of the first."

OSWALD J. SMITH

4

I WILL NOT CHEAT IN ANYTHING, PERSONAL OR PROFESSIONAL

(CARL)

You know you've hit the world of crime big-time when you get a type of crime named after you. That's what happened to Charles Ponzi. I doubt that when he first used the technique of using new investment money to pay what appeared to be miraculously huge rates of return to existing customers, good ol' Charlie had any idea that those types of crime would be for ever known as "doing a Ponzi". In fact, the technique had first been described years previously in Charles Dickens' *Little Dorrit*. It's just that Charlie did it for real and took it to a whole new level.

It's what, in more recent times, Bernard Madoff did. He was so convincingly deceptive that he took in literally scores of the rich and famous, including Hollywood stars. Amazingly, as far as the FBI can tell, no one else in the office knew what was going on, not even his own sons who were directors in the firm. The capacity for a man to conceal the dark side is phenomenal. So big was the sixty-four *billion* dollar fraud that it sent shock waves around the world and has been credited with accelerating the global economic downturn. Not bad for a law school drop-out, son of a plumber. For Bernie it landed him 150 years in a federal prison, where I'm sure he has plenty of time to reflect on his crimes.

Still, at least he can thank the judge that he didn't get as long as Chamoy Thipyaso who, according to the *Guinness Book of Records*, in 1989 got the world's longest sentence for corporate fraud, a staggering 141,078 years.

In recent years the world has been hit with stories of financial scandals that are so breathtakingly huge, they are harder to take in than an anti-malaria tablet! And that's the thing. Cheating and fraud are now such an everyday occurrence that it's only when commonly trusted people cheat, such as ministers of religion, that we get to hear about the small-scale stuff. It now has to be a billion-dollar crime to hit the papers.

Of course it's not just financial cheating that wrecks lives. Again, we only hear about the sensational stuff, such as the bigamist who has a wife in Shetland and a wife and kids in the Isles of Scilly, with both wives convinced that the husband just has to be away a lot for "business".

These stories feed our imagination. We feel a kind of morbid fascination with the details and wonder how on earth the bloke had the audacity to pull it off. We wonder how he afforded it and had the energy for two families. As for bog-standard normal adultery, well that's just not news. After all, everyone's at it. Right?

The simple truth is, whether it's fiddling your expenses, flirting a bit too far with the colleague at work, or a full-blown fraud or an adulterous relationship, your life and others' lives will get damaged. That's as inescapable as death and taxes.

Take the classic example of the office affair. Sex with your wife is almost non-existent; you row about the kids if you have them, or about having kids if you don't. You get moaned at for not being attentive around the home or not showing enough interest in your wife's life.

And then a woman appears on the horizon, wearing a miniskirt and being all attentive to you. She "gets" you. She appreciates your wit, your skills, and your masculinity. You start to make sure you have your breaks at the same time in the office, or somehow always end up having lunch together. When you and your colleagues go out for drinks, you are always the last to leave... together.

And then one time it happens. You have a snog when no one's looking, and let your hands wander. Embarrassed, you both pull away, until the next time, when it goes a stage further.

This might continue for years, but every time you look at your wife a bit of you dies inside. Perhaps things don't improve with your wife and you feel even more driven into the arms of your lover. Then one day you will wake up next to the new lusty love of your life – and she will tell you off because you didn't put the rubbish out in time, or put the toilet seat down...

Most people start off cheating because they are stressed, covetous, jealous, or addicted to sex, or have numbed their moral compass by flirting with areas of grey for too long.

It gets worse. The very nature of cheating means that you then have to live a part of your life in the darkness, which in and of itself corrupts your heart.

In the end you either just get caught or you get ill. You might know of one or two cheats who are apparently prospering on the outside, but I guarantee that the inside will be dark, bitter, and full of angst.

So my advice for a good night's sleep and a healthy heart? Keep a clean conscience. A wise man once said, "Let your yes be yes and your no be no." I might add: "In the long term, cheatin' just ain't worth it."

I need to be completely honest at this point. There are times when I just have to grit my teeth and hold the line with every bit of strength I can muster. Sometimes I can feel so tempted it would be easy just to roll over. I struggle just like every man, and I have to roll up my sleeves and fight. I wish I was so holy I was past all that, but the fact is I have a penis and a pulse. That makes me part of the human race and that means I could get taken out. The truth, however, is that the more you win the battles that no one sees, the bigger the public victories will be. That's a fact.

Here is a dream. What if Codelife could be a kind of "Kingdom kitemark", a mark of quality? Imagine a Codelife plumber, accountant, or policeman. What if you knew that the person you were dealing with was, like you, a man of the Code? He won't cheat you, he doesn't back-stab, and he won't stitch you up. You know that if he slips up, he will admit it and sort the problem out.

So how about it? Could we make this happen across the UK – across the States – across the world? Can we start an enduring movement of men who stand strong and tall for what is right, noble, good, and true? I hope so, for Jesus' sake and for the glory and fame of His Kingdom.

Prayer

God in heaven, stir up a movement of men across the world who spend their lives in pursuit of righteousness and Your Kingdom. Stir men's hearts to live a life worthy of the sacrifice You made. Spare us from mediocrity, half-measures, apathy, religion, and time-wasting nonsense. Send us out and lead us on. In Jesus' name. Amen.

"All good is hard. All evil is easy. Dying, losing, cheating, and mediocrity is easy. Stay away from easy."

SCOTT ALEXANDER

5

I WILL LOOK AWAY FROM THE GUTTER BUT BE PREPARED TO PULL PEOPLE OUT OF IT

(IAN)

One amazing day, 2,000 years ago, as recorded in John's Gospel chapter nine, Jesus met a man who was in the gutter and knew it. He was a beggar who was blind, but the eyes of his heart were working fine. He looked the right way, towards Jesus, and Jesus got him out of the gutter.

They met some Bible-believing religious and community leaders. These men were in their own gutter, but they couldn't see it. They stayed there. That was part of the reason why Jesus rescued the beggar – to teach them and the rest of history a lesson using a visual aid we will never forget. Jesus broke their society's rules and gave the blind man his sight back – and then all hell broke loose. Read the story for yourself.

Jesus' disciples looked at the man and saw an interesting theological problem: what is the cause of suffering in this world? The religious people saw a morally filthy untouchable and chucked him out of their world. The man's own parents looked at their son, saw an embarrassing threat, and said, "You're on your own, son."

Jesus just saw a man and turned him into a miracle, brave enough to pour sarcasm over the religious leaders and show them up for the blind fools they were.

A few years later, Paul (himself a murdering persecutor of the church, transformed by meeting Jesus) released a slave girl from spiritual bondage and exploitation. Her owners didn't like it. Paul and his mate Silas got beaten up and thrown into prison without a trial. There was an earthquake, the prison doors flew open, and the shackles snapped. The head jailer thought he would be taking the rap from the governor and tried to commit suicide. Then he and his family got converted, and Paul and Silas got a public apology and a personal escort to freedom from the magistrates who put them in prison.

Result! Read about it in Acts 16.

Big things happen to people and society when God, with or without our help, pulls people out of gutters. God give *me* the bottle to get on the case – and to be prepared for the consequences!

What is a "gutter" in today's world? I put "trafficking" into the search engine. The top four of the 349,000 results were not *about* trafficking but were sites that would allow *me* to become part of the industry – to "date girls", meet "locals for sex", meet "beautiful Russian women" and "be kinky". God help me. I looked away from the gutter, didn't click on any links, and moved on.

As reported in June 2010 by Amnesty International, there were some 5,000 trafficked people in the UK, according to a government estimate. This is likely to include people being exploited for forced labour as well as people being exploited for the sex industry. London's Metropolitan Police estimate that a trafficked woman in forced prostitution in London "services" somewhere around twenty to thirty men *a day*. These women must wonder sometimes whether they're still human or whether they've just become a living piece of meat on their owner's butcher's slab. In 2008 there was said to be one dedicated safe house providing specialist care for victims of trafficking in the whole of London. It had twenty-five places.

Sometimes, you'd think the whole world was a gutter. Go to the Tearfund website (www. tearfund.org) and follow World News for sobering insights. In the Democratic Republic of Congo, at least 200,000 women have been sexually assaulted over the last decade and more, in an internal conflict where rape has been systematically used as a weapon of war. It's a cliché but no less true that every single component in this huge statistic is a unique person, as valuable as you or me, with their own heartbreaking account. This is one story from the website:

> *Sarah, aged 37, has seen rape, torture, and murder. Rebel forces came one day to the village where she lived with her husband and three children. She recounts: "There were lots of attacks against people by the rebel soldiers. They even dug holes and buried people alive. They told people to have sex with their partners in the presence of everyone, even to have sex with their own brothers and sisters. If we didn't do that, they would kill us." Sarah was raped but survived, though she was injured. There was no immediate help for her in the aftermath. Her husband has since rejected her and kept two of her children.*

> *She is being helped now by Christians. She says now of her attackers, "I have a very strong faith. I have forgotten everything already. I have forgiven them. If I don't forgive them, I won't be free."*

The letter to the Hebrews in the New Testament says of some of history's heroes of faith that "the world was not worthy of them" (Hebrews 11:38). I don't know Sarah, but she seems like one of them to me.

"Come off it," you say. "Anybody can bash us over the head with all these depressing facts. What on earth can I realistically do about all the world's massive problems?"

That's exactly what I think when somebody loads *me* with the same stuff. Up go my defence mechanisms, or I'd go under:

> *"It was different in biblical and historic times. You just knew the people in your village and you were all more or less materially equal. You could spare a bit to help out occasionally when needed. Now with the web and the media, I can stare at the needs of the whole planet from my iPhone. It's different."*

> *"In the developed world, we need more resources to maintain a reasonable existence in our society. In the Third World life is simpler. They're happy with less. It's different."*

> *"It's no use giving out of a sense of duty. God doesn't need our money. The Lord loves a cheerful giver. I'm not yet 'cheerful' about giving more time or money."*

"I can't be responsible for everybody's exploitation and persecution. Am I my brother's keeper?" (Genesis 4:9)

Are these reasonable defence mechanisms, or just me hardening my heart? Jesus told uncompromising stories, such as the one about a rich man ignoring the poor man in the gutter at his gate (Luke 16:19–31). Guess where the rich man went when he died. And the people who, faced with lots of gutter-dwellers, just left them there... and on the day of judgment Jesus says to them, "It was really *Me* you left there," and He herds them together like goats, and leads them – guess where (Matthew 25:31–46).

I've heard preachers make some of these and similar stories seem less uncompromising – saying, for example, "They're not primarily about how much time or money or emotional effort you give away, they're really about having the right attitude to God and being saved by trusting in Him."

Yeah, but I've an uncomfortable feeling that as far as Jesus is concerned, it's all part and parcel of the same thing – uncompromising saying number 893-B: "By their *fruit* you will recognise them" (Matthew 7:20). Let's stop playing games with the Christian faith.

Prayer

Dear God, batter my hard heart with Your uncompromising truth until it breaks, until the love of Christ compels me (2 Corinthians 5:14). I won't like it. It seems so risky, so "unwise" in the world's eyes. Whatever will my friends think about my "wasting" my comfort, time, money, effort, and peace of mind on the gutter? What, even, will some of my family think? Please ram some steel into my spine, because I'm scared. Please get me involved in at least something and let me leave the rest of the issue to You. Please turn me, however painful the journey, in the end into that man which only You can create – a truly cheerful giver.

"Since when do you have to agree with people to defend them from injustice?"

LILLIAN HELLMAN

6

I WILL KEEP MY BODY FIT AND FREE FROM ALL ADDICTIONS

(IAN)

Suppose you're a soldier in one of the world's best special forces units. It's held in awe by its allies and hated but feared by its enemies. It's known for its fearless courage and ruthless efficiency, but also its solid self-discipline. It protects the weak and shows mercy to its prisoners. It owes its values and much of its reputation to its founder. He's a world-renowned figure of towering strength and force of personality.

You go with your squad as military advisors to a third-world wreck of a country which needs your help. The squad gets off the plane in full battledress at a flyblown airstrip and meets the reception committee. The first thing you do is complain that the food on the plane wasn't up to your gourmet standards. The squad moans when they have to march to the camp. You say you normally travel in an air-conditioned coach with video screens and a bar and you were expecting a five-star hotel, not a camp. Some of your squad get short of breath on the march, they're so overweight. The rest complain to the barefooted escort that their boots hurt.

Next morning you meet their bloated, over-decorated old generals. When they ask your opinion on fighting tactics, they all fall about laughing at your answers. You can't understand why. We can. The impression you made the previous day has gone before you. The real you has ruined your unit's reputation. Your walk has killed your talk. The fat old generals, con-artists, themselves, to a man, have seen through you. They know you're really the same as them, only you can't see it yet – which is why they think it's so funny.

So what? You're probably not in the SAS. But you may be a soldier in a sort of revolutionary guerrilla unit called "the followers of Jesus". That illustration about the squad could apply to lots of issues, but what about these things, which really happened?

I was giving a talk to a group of believing men and their non-believing mates. It was about what an adventure following Jesus is – all about taking risks and living on the edge for Him. Before the talk there was a meal.

Suddenly I'm surrounded by vast Christian men stuffing themselves with vast plates of food, followed by equally vast puddings. My neighbour, from behind a food mountain, tells me of his trips to the Third World. Another tells us jokingly that the doctor has just told him he's got type two diabetes. He doesn't know how he's got that, he says.

I couldn't do the food justice (despite raised eyebrows from my neighbour on the other side), partly because I would have fallen asleep in the middle of my own talk, and partly because it just didn't seem to fit the message. The talk would be killed by the walk – "Come and hear about a life of challenge, discipline, sacrifice, and adventure for Jesus' sake. And eat yourself to death at the same time."

Not long ago a church member nearly died from a heart attack. The church prayed for healing, and everybody (including him, I'm sure) gave thanks when he got better. A few weeks later I saw him and his wife at a conference, both grossly overweight, tucking in to their full English fry-ups.

If I've got a bee in my bonnet about this and if I feel smug and superior because I'm fit, then I'm just a health Pharisee (the Pharisees killed Jesus, remember) and I'm in danger of the fate of a Pharisee. I know I'm a failure in all sorts of terrible ways of my own and I'm accepted by Jesus despite them.

But let's get real. Sometimes things have to be said, not because of my or your prejudice, but because of the unit's and, more importantly, the leader's reputation. I'm not talking here of people who are unfit for medical reasons totally beyond their control. I'm talking about the Big Taboo. The thing that, even more than porn, you don't talk about openly in polite Christian circles, the thing that hardly ever gets preached on. It's too embarrassing, too common, too in your face. It's not evangelical PC.

Think about it. In evangelical churches we tend to disapprove of people who smoke, for instance. The poor so-and-sos can't often hide it. It's in the open. And we talk more about kids who get openly hammered and puke all over the cops outside the club on a Saturday night than we do about ourselves when we have too much red wine at home, when we're stressed out. But strangely, there's one really open thing that, because it's so widespread, we've decided to have a head-in-the-sand, let's-not-mention-it, agreement on.

It's the *epidemic of eating far too much* (and taking far too little exercise, just to make things worse).

Let's not look at other people. Let's just look at ourselves. For some of us, family, work, and life seem to take over our health. It seems difficult, but life with Jesus isn't supposed to be a life of excuses. We've been given a spirit of power, of love, and of self-discipline. Some of us need to ask, "What's the deep need in our lives that we're filling with food instead of with following Jesus?"

Or, if we are brutally honest, is it just laziness and greed that are slowly destroying our (and therefore His) body, shortening our life in His service, and making a joke of our witness, and we just can't be bothered to do anything about it?

If you find this article annoys you, listen to what the apostle Paul said about people with this attitude: "...their god is their stomach, their glory is in their shame. Their mind is on earthly things" (Philippians 3:19).

Being addicted to food – probably the commonest addiction in the western world – and being a couch potato may not be much different in God's eyes to being addicted to porn. It's just more acceptable to the church. But of course, in case I start feeling smug again just because, by God's mercy, up to now I've escaped the clutches of the internet, I can be lustful watching the telly, looking at magazine shop shelves and staring down girls' cleavages and at their backsides. And as I write this, on a long rail journey, having I changed trains and walked along platforms full of beautiful women, I realize again that I fail all the time and totally depend on His mercy.

So start dealing with it. Admit any addictions to a trusted Christian friend. Pray with them. Get them to keep asking you about it. Use a specialist organization to help you. Let's not be a slave to *any* of these addictions, whether it's laziness/greed or the opposite, being a fitness fanatic (not a problem for most blokes), sex addiction, gambling, being a workaholic, an alcoholic, an adrenaline junkie, smoking – whatever.

Our only hope is to become completely hooked on something even more powerful. Let's fill our lives and exhaust ourselves, being slaves and addicts to taking risks for Jesus. It's more satisfying, it's safer in the long (eternal) run, and it's the only way we can ever be free. In the case of inactivity and gluttony, it's freedom from avoidable diseases and freedom to live a longer, healthier life, doing the amazing things God has planned for us.

Prayer

Heavenly Father, give me the grit and determination to keep my body and mind fit and free from addiction. Stab my conscience when I make excuses or feel tempted to get lazy and do nothing. Help me to keep my mind pure and my lust in check. I want to be an example for You, a living, breathing example of a man whose life has been touched by the Creator of the universe. So this day and every day, help me to be the man I know I ought to be and help me to have loads of fun along the way so that I actually enjoy it! Amen.

"Those who do not find time
for exercise will have to find
time for illness."

ANON

7

I WILL PUT THE WELFARE OF THOSE CLOSEST TO ME BEFORE MY OWN WELFARE

(ANDY)

If you've just read the title of this chapter and are thinking of skipping it, I'll forgive you. In fairness, you're probably only feeling exactly how I am as I write it: daunted, challenged, and only too aware of your shortcomings and self-centredness.

I started looking out for my own welfare at a young age. I think I was one – one day old, that is. I cried – loudly. Food, cuddles, comfort, whatever it was I needed, I cried for it, and I didn't stop until I got it. And of course, you were probably the same. Inevitably, as I grew up, my ability to look out for myself became more sophisticated. First I learnt that crying + flailing = tantrum, very effective in the supermarket queues. Then I discovered that toys + flailing = weapon, very effective against other toddlers, until I took on one too big for me and had my collarbone handed to me in two pieces.

Before long I, again like you, found myself in the adult world with an arsenal of effective means at my disposal for getting what I wanted: power plays, emotional manipulation, intimidation, bullying, cliques, basically all the stuff Shakespeare wrote about. To make matters really complicated, I wasn't the only one wielding those powerful tools. Everyone else was too.

Living in a world like this makes it really difficult to get what you want. It's as if you're in a constant tug-of-war with the bloke next to you, and he's in a tug-of-war with the bloke next to him, and as you look around, you see that actually the whole world is at it. Everyone wants to win, but no one ever thinks that to have a winner you have to have a loser, and the loser might be them. It's like the 100,000 people lining up to win *The X Factor* each year. For 99,999 it just isn't going to happen, but everyone thinks they'll be the lucky one. It's just like a massive, crazy tug-of-war that the nation loves watching, as if the Colosseum of ancient Rome were back, but with less blood and loads more crying.

At this point we have to ask, "Is this God's best? Is this really how He intended the world to be, how He created us to behave and interact, how He imagined we would be happiest?"

In fact if Jesus is anything to go by – and He is – then God's best for the world is exactly the opposite of the tug-of-war scenario.

Jesus was born into the world and from day one He let go of the rope. He could have had a palace, but He chose a stable. He could have been born to money, but had to work for a living. He could have courted fame, but frequently avoided the crowds. He could have been popular, but made truth more important than adulation. He could have made everyone His servants, but instead looked to find friends that would last. His ultimate act on earth was not one of winning and leaving everyone else on the scrap heap, but of losing *for* the scrap heap so that everyone on it could become a winner.

It was among those closest to Him that He demonstrated most powerfully His unyielding mission to lift up others even at the expense of His own welfare. Amidst the pain of the cross, He looked after His mother. After Peter betrayed Him, Jesus reinstated Peter. Most humbling of all, He faced head-on the night terrors of Gethsemane – even to the point of sweating blood – that you and I might have the opportunity to be called friends of God. Jesus set a new standard for how human beings can behave. Instead of pulling against each other, we could pull together.

The apostle Paul talks in more depth about what this looks like in our own lives, in our families, in the church, and in the world. He speaks powerfully to men, exhorting us to "lay down our lives for our wives", not to "exasperate our children", and to all Christians to "look not only to their own needs, but also the needs of others". In Philippians 2:3 he sums this up by saying, "Do *nothing* out of selfish ambition or vain conceit, *but in humility consider others better than yourselves.*"

What a challenge!

Of course, it starts at home. The people we live with know what we are really like. As men, are we using our strength to get our own way? Are we stepping over our loved ones to get what we want out of life? Are we making others live according to our needs, our wants, our agenda? Can we say that we are truly looking to the welfare of those closest to us above our own?

There's another wonderful verse about Jesus in Hebrews 12:2. It says that "for the joy set before him, he endured the cross". Now the cross was very, very hard and painful. What joy could possibly be talked about here? The joy that Jesus received was that of a family of people, won because of the cross, who are now friends of God.

This same joy is ours to receive as we lay down our lives for those around us. As we let go of the rope, we find that we are pulling against others less and less, and pulling with them more and more. The isolation and loneliness that come from being out for number one are replaced by a true sense of family and belonging. It's even possible to feel relationships you thought tired and stale becoming new, deep, and fulfilling. Such is the power of doing things God's way.

If you want to know where to start, why don't you begin by letting go? Pray, and let God guide you. The truth is all of us are pulling on a lot of ropes with a lot of people. Letting go of them all can take a lifetime, but we can start by letting go of an attitude, a goal, a behaviour or a focus, and daily letting go until one day we realize that that particular rope is gone. And ask those near you how you can pull alongside them rather than against them. You may be surprised by the answers you get and just how life-changing this attitude is.

And also think about this: what's the alternative – to keep living for number one? What a miserable existence that is. It's not how God made you to be, and you'll never find happiness that way.

Be a man like Jesus and lift up those around you, even if and when it makes your own life hard. Do it because it makes the world a better place, you a better person, your loved ones happier people, and most of all the name of Jesus honoured wherever you are. And may the joy of Jesus be your experience and your inheritance.

Prayer

Heavenly Father, make me a man of sacrifice and not self-gain.

Read Isaiah 58 and Luke 4:18.

"Maybe I was brave,
I don't know. At the time I
was just doing the job;
I didn't have time for other
thoughts."

PRIVATE JOHNSON BEHARRY VC

8

I WILL TREAT ALL MEN AND WOMEN AS BROTHERS AND SISTERS

(ANDY)

I grew up with most of my extended family living on the other side of the world. Cousins, grandparents, aunties, and uncles were all faceless entities my parents forced me to talk to on Christmas Day. Phrases such as "Thanks for the socks", "What's the weather like in England?", "Nice to talk to you" were rehearsed and performed with practised ease, but truth be told, I wasn't really feeling it.

At the age of 18 I left Australia for the UK and for the first time met the whole family. Something took me completely by surprise: I actually liked them! I found all kinds of areas of similarity, from preferences in food to the things that made us laugh, and I realized that I enjoyed being with them. I was going beyond simply knowing who my family were to feeling a special attachment to them.

We don't all feel a whole lot of love for our families, but most of us agree that it's the ideal that we should.

So far so good. You think I'm going to say that we all need to feel this kind of love for the whole world, and in part you're right, but there's something more we need to understand first.

Many people feel a fierce loyalty to their own families, and this can be a good thing, but the problem begins when this loyalty and love impedes their ability to love those outside their own family. To understand this problem, we need to understand how we all develop in terms of how we think about others.

During the "terrible twos", infants are almost completely besotted with themselves, striving to get what they want. Of course it's different for each child, but every parent will tell you that they have their work cut out teaching the importance of thinking about others.

Hopefully, over time the child learns that they are part of a community of people and have to contribute in order to enjoy the benefits of that community, so they wash up, do their homework, act politely, and stop having tantrums... hopefully. Parents judge this training a success when the child grows up to care for their own family, friends, and perhaps even community or nation, with adult selflessness.

So what could be wrong with this? Nothing, unless you don't happen to be from the same family, community or nation – as when Andy walked into a London pub during a televised Australia–England rugby game and yelled out when the Aussies scored a try. On that occasion he got away with it because he left the pub sharpish, but for most of the history of the human race, people haven't been so lucky. War, slavery, subjugation, and even genocide have all come about because we've felt that it's OK to act like the terrible two-year-old when someone outside our community has something we want or has just cheesed us off. Read the history books for five minutes and you'll find all the evidence you need.

So what does God think of this? Unsurprisingly, it's not what you'd call His "Plan A". Adam turned against Eve, and then bad went to much worse when Cain turned against Abel. By the time of Noah, God was grieved with the whole world.

When we get to Abraham, God has a new plan of action, and in its simplicity lies its genius: one man is called to get to know God, and he in turn will instruct his family, who in turn will instruct the world (Genesis 12:1–3). This isn't self-centred living, or even family- or nation-centred living. This is world-centred living.

Of course, we know how things went.

God's people can't even handle Plan B, and thankfully it's OK. God's master plan, His AAA strategy, is to come into the world Himself to show us how to really behave. Jesus touches people with leprosy, speaks to Samaritans, forgives prostitutes, and loves everyone. He dies forgiving the very people who killed Him, and then leaves His Spirit after the resurrection and ascension as a gift for (mind-blowingly for the time) anyone who follows Him. Jew, non-Jew, female, male, African, European, and even Australian... nobody is excluded.

Christianity spreads like wildfire, and as in all growing families there are tensions. The New Testament gives us many accounts of arguments and disagreements. Some people like one leader and not another, some people show favouritism, some people believe that you have to do certain things to receive God's grace, and some are even taking each other to court because of their disputes.

With all of this going on we see two things said again and again and again. First, God's people are told to love each other – lots. Second, they are told to look outwards and live lives that attract people to God: in a sense, to live out the mission Abraham received centuries earlier.

They're reminded that in a world where dog

eats dog they're called to a higher standard. In 1 Timothy, Paul exhorts Timothy to treat his church people like fathers, sons, daughters, and mothers, and of course this is actually a call for each one of us. In fact, we're called to treat other Christians as family, and the rest of the world as potential family, because God wants everyone to be saved (John 3:16).

If you get this in your head, it changes everything. If you agree that the ideal is to feel great about your family and treat them well, and if you agree that God calls us to see each other as family or potential family, then no one can be treated as a second-class citizen. Your ideal standards for family in terms of violence, anger, and even sexual behaviour become the standard for how you treat everyone. In fact, let me put it a better way: *God's ideal standards for family become the standard for how you treat everyone.*

It's what Jesus had in mind when He told the parable of the Good Samaritan. He was basically saying, "Think of the person you feel you have the most right to marginalize, and now listen to this – you don't have any right, because God loves them and sees that you and they are the same."

This means there is no excuse to treat the people at work one way and those at home another. Moaning about immigrants because of their ethnicity, belittling or abusing the opposite sex because they're just an object, writing off the other side of the world because it's too difficult to understand the complexity of their problems, or just adding to the world's pain through our own ignorance – none of it is OK.

Like it or not, you and I are family, and we're charged with demonstrating this to the world. Let's act in such a way that others see that being a part of God's family through Jesus – treating everyone as brothers and sisters – really is the answer to the age-old problem of people hurting people.

Prayer

Father, deliver me from the insecurities and bad attitudes that lead me to be less than a good man. Help me to look beyond myself to the needs of others. If You see anything in me that is rubbish, if I sulk, bully, rage, or dominate, then show me. See if there is anything offensive in me and lead me in the way everlasting. Amen.

"This is my command: Love
one another."

JESUS CHRIST OF NAZARETH

9

I WILL LEAD AS HE WOULD LEAD. I WILL HONOUR MY LEADERS PROVIDED THIS ALSO HONOURS HIM. I WILL FOLLOW HIM IN COMPANY WITH MY SISTERS AND BROTHERS

(ANDY)

I once worked as a temp. It wasn't a great time in my life, but it was necessary – I was completely broke. For the princely sum of £5 an hour I did any office work going. I filed, answered phones, did data entry: it was a real hoot. At one office where I worked for six months I was one temp among dozens.

We were working for a mobile phone carrier (not mentioning any names) and were racked along a line of desks like the rowers from *Ben Hur*. Instead of oars we had keyboards, and instead of a drummer we had a line manager.

She was murder. She strolled up and down the aisle, peering over our shoulders every five minutes to make sure we were working at 110 per cent. The phones constantly rang, and our stats were up in neon lights. If you didn't answer the calls in time and then finish them quickly you were berated by the slave master. It was miserable.

About six months in, people started to get laid off. We were temps, so there was no golden handshake; in fact there was a golden five minutes when you were told to pack your bags, and then you were out the door. One girl was told to go and was really upset. She even cried; she desperately needed the money. My heart went out to her, so like Oliver Twist I dared to get up from my seat, move away from the desk, and head towards the Dragon.

Boldly I made her an offer: I could go instead of the girl, and she could have my job. We were both good workers and it was fair, or so I thought. Big mistake! Our line manager bored into me with her gaze, and then a thin-lipped smile presented itself on her face. We were both sacked.

I've known a lot of leaders, and am glad to report that I've worked under some awesome managers, but this wasn't one of those times. My six months at this particular firm gave me an "up close and personal" insight again into how bullying and autocracy can run amok within power structures. Whenever I see bad leadership I'm amazed at the short-sightedness. It's obvious, isn't it? You get the best from people when you treat them well.

In fact, if the mark of a good leader is the wellbeing of the followers, Jesus was the ultimate manager. He took a ragtag bunch of guys and turned them into world-changers. If we're leading and/or being led (in fact it's usually both, in one way or another), we could do a lot worse than check out His style.

Jesus was never on an ego trip, never played power games to cement His position, never developed factions or entertained infighting. As we read in Philippians 2, He took the nature of a servant and humbled Himself for a greater cause. When He led, it was with the authority of One who spoke words of life. Most importantly, His security came from knowing where He had come from and where He was going (John 13:1–3).

And that's the answer, really. Good leaders – and good followers – are all about being secure. Knowing that we belong to God, are loved by Him, and are a part of His great eternal plan negates the need to carve out our own little niche in life. I can seek promotion, but getting it or not getting it doesn't define me as a person. I can work under a difficult boss, but their opinion of me is not *the* opinion of me, so instead of rebelling I can remain godly. And when I do have responsibility over others, I can serve them, using what gifts and insights I have to lift them up rather than keep them down. My greatest delight can be in seeing someone I have led eventually surpassing me because they are partly standing on my shoulders.

At church and at work I can honour my leaders because I understand that God has placed them in authority; He is in control, after all. Of course, I can and should stand against ungodly leadership activity – as long as I'm not motivated by personal grievances masquerading as righteous anger. Honouring our leaders means acknowledging that their work is hard, that only they see the big picture and have the pressures they have, that they will be held accountable for their actions one day, and that we are called to make their lives easier, not harder.

We can't achieve this state of being in isolation. The hard knocks of life soon add up, and the relentless gravity of sin drags us towards rebellion, not grace. Before long we can all get frustrated, angry, power-hungry, abusive, and downright nasty. That's when we need each other.

It's true that iron sharpens iron. It's also good at bursting bubbles. Inflated egos, expanding rebelliousness, and "blown up out of all proportion" anger all need to be nailed with the insightful wisdom of those closest to us in Christ. Left to our own devices, we simply justify ourselves and gather like-minded cronies around us. Surrounded by the godly, we are forced to take stock and get things sorted.

That's why church makes sense, and why it is sometimes a place of difficulty and discomfort. God doesn't call us to be church because it is always easy, but because it glorifies Him – it *should* show the world His goodness.

Maybe as we rub each other up the wrong way we might just happen to rub off some of the bad stuff too! I guess what I'm saying is that when our relationships feel the hardest, God can be doing the most work.

I sometimes wonder about the Dragon. Is she still the way she was? Has she learnt any grace along the way, perhaps even encountered Christ? Maybe I'll never know. Maybe right now she's yelling at another hapless employee.

What I do know about is *me*. The people *I* am leading right now. The people *I* am being led by. The company of Christians God has called *me* to be among at this time.

I have to ask myself: am I secure enough in Christ? Is there honour in my actions? Am I genuinely walking with my brothers and sisters?

Between myself, God, and a few select friends, I'm going to keep asking these questions. How about you?

Prayer

Father, help me to be a leader who lays down his life for others. Help me to be a leader who serves and seeks the best for those around me. Help me to honour authority and to make the lives of those who lead me easier, not harder. Amen.

"When I was young there was no respect for the young, and now that I am old there is no respect for the old. I missed out coming and going."

J. B. PRIESTLEY

10

I WILL USE MY STRENGTH TO PROTECT THE WEAK AND STAND AGAINST THE CRUEL USE OF POWER

(CARL)

Ever heard of Ioseb Besarionis dze Jughashvili? This is a good one for a pub quiz, so stay with me.

He was born in 1878 and became one of the most feared men to walk planet earth in the twentieth century. Got it yet?

OK, you probably know him better as Josef Stalin. From 1929 to 1953 he ruled the Soviet Union with an iron fist. In fact, the term "iron fist" is probably an understatement.

It's estimated by historians that anywhere between a horrifying 600,000 and 1.5 million ordinary people, just like you and me, were executed in the so called "great purge" which was Stalin's attempt to "purify" the Soviet Union. It doesn't stop there.

His rule also saw millions (some suggest as many as 9 million people) die from imprisonment, forced resettlement to famine areas, and general repression. Millions more died from national food shortages and the consequences of an oppressive regime.

Of course, millions also died in World War II as both combatants and civilians. Soldiers were often sent into battle sharing weapons or used as "trampler" units to clear minefields.

So that's Josef Stalin. An absolute ruler, responsible, it is said, for the deaths of millions, perhaps tens of millions, of men, women, and children. Maybe more than the population of the United Kingdom, certainly more than the population of England. You just can't get your head round it, can you?

A story is told about an encounter Stalin had with a chicken while relaxing at his retreat in Georgia with his leaders. It's said that while struggling to get his team to understand the relationship between control and power, he grabbed a chicken and started to pull fistfuls of feathers from it.

Needless to say, the chicken fought back, but Stalin kept ripping the feathers out. To everyone's amazement, once it was bare of feathers it stopped fighting and became still, trying to press itself into Stalin's body. It even followed him around the courtyard when he threw grain on the floor.

Deprived of all protection from the cold, the chicken now needed Stalin's body heat to stay warm... and was also dependent on him for food. "This is how we lead the people," he is said to have calmly remarked to his stunned audience. "Take what they need from them, and they will always follow us for food."

And that's what he did. He terrorized the nation. Millions had their property taken by the Communist Party, and the population lived under constant threat of torture, execution, or exile. As a consequence they had no choice but to peacefully submit in order just to survive.

History is littered with power abusers like Stalin. Pol Pot killed over a quarter of his countrymen. Idi Amin was said, among other things, to be a cannibal. Caligula made his horse a consul and priest. Nero executed his mother and adopted brother, and is rumoured to have played the fiddle while Rome burned to the ground. Then there are others such as Hitler, or Attila the Hun. The list is long.

In 1887 Lord Acton coined the now famous phrase on power: "Power tends to corrupt, and absolute power corrupts absolutely."

The thing is, however, that the Bible tells us that there is one who has absolute power, but he has never wielded it like an Idi Amin or a Josef Stalin.

When Jesus walked on the planet some 2,000 years ago He demonstrated the true exercise of absolute power not by using a sword, or fear, murder, mayhem, torture, manipulation, and butchery. He exercised power by laying His life down with nails through His wrists.

At any time in His life He could have called on more power than we can ever comprehend. But He didn't. Instead He gave life to the dead and dying, healed the sick, spent time with scumbags and villains, protected the weak, and ultimately gave up His life.

So does power corrupt? It surely can, but not if we live by the code of honour that the Bible gives us.

What the world needs is men of honour who choose the path of sacrifice, not self-gain. From the employee who fiddles expenses, or the police officer who goes that little bit over the top, to the manager who bullies the weakest worker, things must change.

So here's the rub. That means practically that you use your life to give life to others and not to take it from them. It means that what influence you do have, whether that's with family, your mates, or your work colleagues, you use for the greater good.

You use your influence to encourage people to do better than you. You are the one who apologizes first. You take the hit on behalf of others. It means not playing games in the office and manipulating a situation so you come out on top. It means using your words to build up, not to destroy. It means being a peacemaker of the type that is prepared to put themselves in harm's way to bring peace. Just like Jesus did.

And when we fail, which we will, we pick ourselves up, dust ourselves down, and press on. We have resurrection DNA! But more of that in the final chapter.

Prayer

Heavenly Father, give me Your heart for justice. I do not want to be a man who looks the other way, but a man who spends himself on behalf of others and fights for the widow, orphan, and marginalized. Show me today, in my daily life, how to make a difference and to leave traces of the Kingdom wherever I go and in whatever I do. Amen.

"The ultimate tragedy is not the oppression and cruelty by the bad people but the silence over that by the good people."

MARTIN LUTHER KING, JR

11

I WILL PROTECT THE WORLD THAT GOD HAS MADE

(IAN)

What do you think about these emails?

Hi, Dad! Things are much better since you got this flat for me and my brother. I don't know what would have happened without it. It's crap being on the streets in winter, what with Pete being disabled etc. Honest, the problem wasn't me. I got let down by everybody. I should have let you know the state we were in sooner, but I guess I was too proud. Now we've got this great pad, I can get work and I can make it this time. Nobody gives you a chance if you haven't got a fixed address. Don't worry about Pete, I'll look after him. I know this is our last chance. I know I've messed up before, but not this time. I'm sooooo grateful. Please keep the rent cheques coming. Love you lots. Dave.

Dad, dont lisen to dave he dont let me yuse the computer but ees out. Ees trashin the flat, partyin an ees yusin the rent money on skank. Ee dont giv me ardly any food. We will be chukd out an I will be stufd. Ee ses ee dus but ee dont reely giv a toss. Plees elp me, Peet.

So, what do you think about Dave: self-centred bastard and a loser?

How would you feel if you were Pete: scared, desperate, helpless?

And what would it be like, being Dad and getting the emails out of the blue: a mixture of being gutted and furious?

It's a parable, of course. Dave is a Christian in the western world, trashing the planet through his "normal" but wasteful lifestyle and doing some weird double act in his head with himself and with God. Pete is a farmer with a family, on the coast in Bangladesh, about to be ruined by rising sea levels. The flat is the world and Dad is God. The emails are prayers.

It seems to me that if you are somebody in the western world who calls themselves a follower of Jesus; you fall into one of two camps.

In the first camp, we believe we've been given the planet by our Maker, but either through selfishness, or laziness, or by being stupid or conning ourselves, we're trashing the place and screwing the poor. Some of us are doing the double act and saying to God, "We love you, Lord, but we're trashing the place anyway." We can live with ourselves over this, because deep down inside, without really noticing we've done it, we've decided the poor in the Third World aren't really people – at least, not like we are. Some of us have got a crazy twist to the idea of the new heaven and new earth, and are in effect saying in terms of the parable, "We love you, Dad, and we know you are going to give us another flat one day, so we're trashing this one 'cause it doesn't matter any more and we're screwing Pete in the meantime. You won't mind, will you?"

In the second camp, we believe we've been given the planet by our Maker as a priceless gift to look after and as the home of the poor, and it's somehow cost Him His life to put it right in the end, the same as it has to put us right. The planet and we are on the same journey together. Our destiny is all bound up together with the planet's, in His plan, which is beyond our understanding.

Which camp sounds like it's seeing things the way Jesus sees them? It's a no-brainer.

Let's try facing up to this:

- There is now overwhelming scientific evidence that the world is warming and that human activity is causing the problem. This is through increasing "greenhouse gases" such as carbon dioxide (often shortened to "carbon").

- Warmer oceans will expand, and the Greenland and Antarctic ice caps will start to melt, pouring more water into the expanded seas. The Arctic sea ice will disappear and stop reflecting the sun's heat back into space, and the whole thing will become a vicious circle.

- The latest estimate (March 2009) is that sea levels will rise by an average of 1 to 1.5 metres by 2100. Some of your grandchildren will be around then.

- Winds and tides make the situation much worse in some places. Millions of people near the coast, too poor to move, will be ruined and starved.

- Loss of glaciers and snow will mean water shortages for one-sixth of the world's population, who depend on them for drinking water.

- Warmer seas will cause more storms and flooding, adding to the 140 million people a year who are already affected.

- Other areas will be hotter and drier. There will be more and more intense summers like that of 2003, when 52,000 people in

Europe died as a direct result of the heat.

What can a follower of Jesus do?

First, personally: think "R".

- **Repent**. Acknowledge you were wrong and take your head out of the sand. Start setting things right one at a time, step by step.

- **Refuse** goods and packaging you don't need.

- **Reduce**: electricity, car journeys (use the bus, cycle, or catch the train), heating (insulate, wear warmer clothes).

- **Reuse/repair**, instead of buying new.

- **Recycle** whenever possible and pay for your excess carbon use (known as carbon offsetting: visit www.climatestewards. net[1]).

- **Rethink** how to do things. There are many helpful books – one good one is Ruth Valerio's *L is for Lifestyle*. Visit www. lisforlifestyle.com.

---

1. Ian adds: "I have a special sympathy with the 'Climate Stewards' organisation. My mate and I were once rock climbing, halfway up a 750 foot rock face, when the huge chunk of rock he was climbing simply came free. He fell 100 feet, whizzing past me on the way down. I (and the rock I was attached to) managed to hold him on the rope. He survived, just, but broke both his legs and his shoulder. We were helicoptered off; he was in hospital for three weeks, off work for three months, changed his job and started 'Climate Stewards'. But that's another story."

Second, together: influence your church, if you have one, and your friends: visit www. ecocongregation.org.

Third, let environmental care be part of the way you show the world what Jesus is like: visit www.arocha.org and www.tearfund.org/climate.

Go for it.

Prayer

Father, help me to protect the world that You have made. Help me to be a witness in the way I treat Your creation. Amen.

"The only way to save a rhinoceros is to save the environment in which it lives, because there's a mutual dependency between it and millions of other species of both animals and plants."

DAVID ATTENBOROUGH

12

IF I FAIL, I WILL NOT GIVE UP, AS HE NEVER GIVES UP ON ME

(CARL)

There have been many times so far in life when I have felt like quitting. The funny thing, if I pause to think about when and why, is that the kind of triggers that make me want to quit are pretty much all based on the same thing.

In the last few years I've got into doing a bit of endurance sport.

I've managed to cycle from Land's End to John O'Groats, from Calais to Nice via the Alps, and from Nice to Napoli. Each of these cycling epics was completed in nine days.

In 2010 I ran the London Marathon.

Now, before you start to get the impression that I'm a natural sportsman, let me quickly say that nothing could be farther from the truth! I still carry too much weight and I'm not as fit as I would like to be.

Frankly, I got involved in all this stuff as a response to following Jesus and wanting to honour him with my health. I was also told by a close mate of mine that I was getting unfit and fat (as he cycled past me looking like a Peperami in lycra), which was quite a motivator at the time. Honestly, I found every stage of training and completing the challenges pretty tough, physically and emotionally. There was one occasion when, cycling up a mountain for about three hours solid after having already cycled up various climbs for sixty or so miles that morning, I could have cried if I had let myself. But never once did quitting enter my mind. I'm too bloody-minded for that (even though I was overtaken by a butterfly on one particularly steep section, which was a tad deflating)!

However, I do have my "quit buttons". Being misunderstood or attacked by someone close to me (thankfully a very rare experience) can have me wanting to run to the hills and hide from everything and everyone. People perceive me to be a strong person, and I guess in many ways I do have a large capacity to handle emotional or physical pain, but just like Superman (and I'm not comparing myself here), we all have our kryptonite!

So, what's yours?

Many times over the years I've come across

blokes who have chucked in the towel too early. Sure, they've been on the ropes, but they were still standing and could still have fought their way out of the situation they were in. The problem is, they hadn't paused to think that, just maybe, their quit button was being pressed.

I can think of one guy who had it all going for him but was so consumed with guilt and shame over just a few slip-ups with porn that he was all for running away from everything to do with Jesus and the church. He just couldn't see his way through the shame. He knew the theory of grace, but it hadn't touched his heart.

I can think of another guy who in years gone by had had a powerful vision to set up a charity to help the broken, but because he had hit the wall and faced some stiff opposition he had quit too soon. He was still plagued with feelings of "what might have been" if he hadn't quit so soon.

I could go on with example after example.

I've learned a lesson about vision that's probably worth sharing. It seems to me that there is an eighteen-month time frame when you first get an idea to do something that becomes something of a roller coaster ride. You just need to tough it out. Normally after about eighteen months, a new project or vision hits the wall. It could be lack of funds, people problems, personal sin, or a combination of these and more.

But something special is happening at the same time. God is also trying to shape and fashion both you and the vision. He wants to take out what is not of Him and put more of Himself into it. So many people quit at this point and miss the fact that the blessing is only just round the corner. So if that's you, dig in and keep going on. Whether it's a business you are running, a ministry, or a relationship, the principle holds strong.

They say that the darkest hour is before the dawn. Sometimes we need to remember that, grit our teeth, and get a bit dogged.

The same applies with personal struggles and failure. Don't let the past define your future. God doesn't. For those who walk with Him, it is a truth in the Bible that He will always finish what He started. So that vision you had? That idea? If that was from God, dare to believe that just maybe it's not too late.

Besides all this, we have resurrection DNA. It's a fact that we can be knocked down but never out. Just remember that next time you take a hit. (The declaration in Matthew 28, "He has risen", is the guiding force here.)

I was watching my daughter play football a couple of months ago. In fact it was her first game – and Emily was the only goalkeeper on the team.

During the pre-match warm-up, Emily suddenly turned and started to walk off the pitch, with her coach guiding her with an arm round her shoulders. We don't know whether it was a dodgy breakfast, nerves, or illness, but Emily was feeling pretty sick.

I sat with her for a few minutes, with the game due to start any moment. We had a father/daughter chat. I've always taught my girls never to walk away from a challenge, not to quit too soon, not to say, "I can't."

So I was proud of her when she picked herself up and got on the pitch.

Moments later the worst situation developed. The other team got a penalty. So there was Emily. First ever game, only started training and learning the game a few weeks earlier, aged only 11, standing alone.

Talk about tense. There she is, my little girl standing alone, and I can't take it for her!

The game went into slow motion as the striker ran up and hit the ball hard at the goal. It was a defining moment for Emily as she stood her ground... and saved it – to a massive cheer from the parents of our side.

She faced up and it paid off. Nice one!

My example in all of this is of course Jesus. Sure, I could talk about Ranulph Fiennes or some other amazing explorer, or the entrepreneur who never gave up despite multiple bankruptcies, only to make his millions. But they are nothing compared to Jesus, who held the destiny of the world on His shoulders.

I've often thought about the time in Gethsemane when Jesus stayed up praying before facing the cross. He had to be able to say no in order for it to be a willing sacrifice of His life. But despite the cosmic pressures and spiritual battles, the scale of which we can't fathom, He held the line. It was the same in the desert. So there is our example.

Be men who hold the line. Codelife is a movement of men who don't quit. We don't let up, shut up, or compromise.

One time in my early twenties I hit a really low patch. I remember sitting back in a chair feeling pretty worthless. My rent cheque had bounced, I was out of cash and all my mates were away. In the darkest moment I remember hearing an inner voice, a whisper from the Holy Spirit saying to me, "you were worth dying for son..." That changed everything.

Here is the final word on the matter. If we stuff up, and there is every likelihood that we will, let's simply dust ourselves off, spit out the grit, and get going again as we remember that Jesus by His grace still believes in us. Priceless.

Prayer

Father, I covenant before You that I will not quit or give up. You never gave up on me, and in the same way I will not walk away from the life You called me to. I have resurrection DNA, I am a man with a destiny and a future in God. Thank You that You always finish what You start. Amen.

"Pain is temporary. Quitting lasts forever."

LANCE ARMSTRONG

APPENDIX: THE CODE (LITURGICAL VERSION)

Each of the twelve points of the Code is followed by a prayer, based on and expanding that point.

Jesus is my Captain, Brother, Rescuer and Friend.

You are my Maker. I am Your work in progress.
You are my Rescuer. I have been salvaged.
You paid the price for putting me right and forgiving me, with Your life. All I can do is thank You.
You are my Father. I am Your son.
You are my Owner. I am Your slave.
You are my Captain. I am Your warrior.
You are my Brother. We are brothers.
You are my Friend. We are friends.

I owe everything to Him. I will do anything for Him.

All my time, all my money, all my gifts, all my talents, all my powers of thought, all my energy, and all my strength will be at Your disposal instantly and at all times, because I don't own any of these – they're all Yours.

I will consult You on all my plans for the future and take Your guidance, because You hold my future in Your hands.

I will unashamedly make Him known through my actions and words.

I will make friends with, and share my life with, those who don't know You, because they have to find You through me and they need You even more than I do now.

I will do all these things in Your name, to honour Your name. If asked why I do them, I will say that if there seems anything good in me, I owe it all to You.

I will not cheat in anything, personal or professional.

I will be honest and truthful in all my dealings, because You are the truth and the enemy is the father of all lies.

Provided it doesn't conflict with Your orders, I will obey my government and its laws, because in Your time on earth You said, "Give to Caesar what belongs to Caesar" and You accepted the government's death penalty even when it was unjust.

I will look away from the gutter, but be prepared to pull people out of it.

I will serve and care for all people, but especially those that the world counts as scum, because You were born into a feeding trough, You became a refugee, the "scum" were Your friends, You let a woman with a scandalous reputation worship You as she washed Your feet with her tears, and because You died even for somebody like me.

I will keep my body fit and free from any addictions.

I will not become a slave to any addictions. I am only *Your* slave. It's the only way I can be free.

I will respect and look after my own body. As far as it's up to me, I will keep it fit, because You live in it and use it for Your purposes.

I will put the welfare of those closest to me before my own welfare.

I will lead my family by selfless example, in the way You lead all Your people on earth.

I will only have sex within marriage. That is the way You designed me to behave. If it is Your plan for me to get married (or if I am already married), I will always be faithful to my wife – for her sake, for my children's sake, for *my* sake, and because You always keep Your promises to me.

I will treat all men and women as brothers and sisters.

I will honour and respect women as my mothers, sisters, daughters, and friends, and men as my fathers, brothers, sons, and friends. I will remember that the women stood by You at Your death, when most of the men had fled.

I will lead as He would lead. I will honour my leaders provided this also honours Him. I will follow Him in company with my sisters and brothers.

I will lead by selfless example, in the way You lead all Your people on earth.

I will pay attention to those who lead me in my journey with You, but I will always test them against Your Word, because there are many wolves in sheep's clothing.

I will follow You in the company of other people, not alone, because You gathered a group of friends and through them changed the world. I act only as one part of Your whole body on earth.

I will have at least one other brother of Yours who knows all my weaknesses as well as my strengths, as I know his. We will be accountable to You through each other because only You are strong enough to stand against the enemy alone.

I will use my strength to protect the weak and stand against the abuse of power.

I will protect and care for all children. I will

remember that unless I become like one of them before You, I can't even start to follow You.

I will fight Your battles bravely. You are my strength and my shield. But I will only fight *Your* battles, because although I will fight the enemy I will otherwise seek peace between all people. You are the great peacemaker.

I will protect the world that God has made.

I will protect and care for this broken planet and its resources, because it's Yours, because You gave it to us to care for, because it's the home of the poor, and because the planet and Your people are on the same journey together, to the same destiny, in Your plan.

If I fail I will not give up. He never gives up on me.

I know I will sometimes fall and break this code. I know this will seriously anger, disappoint, and hurt You. But I will always ask Your forgiveness and get up again, and never give up and never look back, but always keep following You, because I know You will forgive me and stay with me and give me strength. I know my problems are nothing compared to the prize. Even the prize is undeserved. It's Your gift and it's certain.

I will keep learning about You and listening
to You through Your Word and by Your Spirit,
and I will keep talking to You. Otherwise our
friendship will grow cold and I will become
useless to You.

With You I will fight to see this through and,
in the end, to know You fully, reach my true
potential, and become Your masterpiece.

I know all these things add up to what You call
love.

I know it's tougher and stronger than anything
and lasts longer than anything.

I will always seek to love just as You do.

THE CODE
(A PERSONAL COMMITMENT)

You are my Maker. I am Your work in progress.

You are my Redeemer. You paid the price for putting me right and forgiving me, with Your life. All I can do is thank You and say that I owe You everything.

You are my Rescuer. I have been salvaged.

You are my Owner. I am Your slave.

You are my Friend. We are friends.

You are my Commander. I am Your warrior.

You are my Brother. We are brothers.

You are my Father. I am Your son.

- I will serve and care for all people, but especially those that the world counts as scum, because You were born into a feeding trough, You became a refugee, the "scum" were Your friends, You let a woman with a scandalous reputation worship You as she washed Your feet with her tears, and because You died even for somebody like me.

- I will make friends with, and share my life with, those who don't know You, because they have to find You through me and they need You even more than I do now.

- I will honour and respect women as my mothers, sisters, daughters, and friends, and men as my fathers, brothers, sons, and friends. I will remember that the women stood by You at Your death, when most of the men had fled.

- I will protect and care for all children. I will remember that unless I become like one of them, before You, I can't even start to follow You.

- I will not become a slave to any addictions. I am only *Your* slave. It's the only way I can be free.

- I will respect and look after my own body. As far as it's up to me, I will keep it fit, because You live in it and use it for Your purposes.

- All my time, all my money, all my gifts, all my talents, all my powers of thought, all my energy, and all my strength will be at Your disposal instantly and at all times, because I don't own any of these – they're all Yours.

- I will consult You on all my plans for the future and take Your guidance, because You hold my future in Your hands.

- I will only have sex within marriage. That is the way You designed me to behave. If it is Your plan for me to get married (or if I am already married), I will always be faithful to my wife – for her sake, for my children's sake, for *my* sake, and because You always keep Your promises to me.

- I will lead my family by selfless example, in the way You lead all Your people on earth.

- I will be honest and truthful in all my dealings, because You are the truth and the enemy is the father of all lies.

- Provided it doesn't conflict with Your orders, I will obey my government and its laws, because in Your time on earth You said, "Give to Caesar what belongs to Caesar" and You accepted the government's death penalty even when it was unjust.

- I will protect and care for this broken planet and its resources, because it's Yours, because You gave it to us to care for, because it's the home of the poor, and because the planet and Your people are on the same journey together, to the same destiny, in Your plan, for ever.

- I will fight Your battles bravely, but only *Your* battles, because although I will fight the enemy I will otherwise seek peace between all people. You are the great peacemaker.

- I will follow You in the company of other people, not alone, because You gathered a group of friends and through them changed the world. I act only as one part of Your whole body on earth.

- I will keep learning about You and listening to You through Your Word and by Your Spirit, and I will keep talking to You. Otherwise our friendship will grow cold and I will become useless to You.

- I will pay attention to those who lead me in my journey with You, but I will always test them against Your Word, because there are many wolves in sheep's clothing.

- I will have at least one other brother of Yours who knows all my weaknesses as well as my strengths, as I know his. We will be accountable to You through each other because only You are strong enough to stand against the enemy alone.

- I know I will sometimes fall and break this code. I know this will seriously anger, disappoint, and hurt You. But I will always ask Your forgiveness and get up again, never give up and never look back, but always keep following You, because I know You will forgive me, stay with me and give me strength. I know my problems are nothing compared to the prize. Even the prize is undeserved. It's Your gift and it's certain.

- I know all these things add up to what You call love. I know it's tougher and stronger than anything and lasts longer than anything. I will love as You do. I will do it in Your name, to honour Your name. If I'm asked why I do these things, I will say that if there seems anything good in me, I owe it all to You.

- With You I will fight to see this through and, in the end, to know You fully, reach my true potential, and become Your masterpiece.

MY RESPONSE TO THE CODE

For each point of the Code I will do the
following:

1. _____

_____

2. _____

_____

3. _____

_____

4. _____

_____

5. _____

_____

6. _____

_____

7.

8.

9.

10.

11.

12.

FIGHTER

A poem written by Carl as a response
from the heart, wanting to live a life of no
compromise.

I want to be a fighter
Not a shallow in the moment receiver
I want to be a grappler
Not a push over yielder –
A weak man
Who cannot stand
Against the first raised hand.
I want to be a God follower
A God botherer
A Jesus freak

I want to be a truth finder
Not a blinded lie receiver
I want to be a truth declarer
Not a silent, weakened, pushover
I want to be a trailblazer
Not just mediocre
A man who stands
Against the tide
No backslider

I want to be a fighter
A deep faith finder
A man who never yields
A man who stands
Against upraised hands

I am a God follower
A God botherer
An enemy scarer
A Jesus freak
A reputation in hell
With a story to tell
I am a fighter, a fire lighter

I may be weak
Sometimes a geek
I may be shy
(And sometimes believe lies)
But I'll be the fighter
A God receiver
A grappler
And an enemy defeater
No compromise

Carl Beech, August 2010

DIGGING DEEPER

For regular evangelistic podcasts on the Code, please go to iTunes and search for "Beechy and Willmott".

Codelife has its own iTunes podcasts, as does CVM.

For more resources, please go to www.codelife.org.

For a good rites of passage course that will lead your young men and sons to Codelife, please look at *Manmade*, available from CVM.

How can I spread the word?

Please post your news and views about Codelife on your blogs, with links back to our website. Post reviews of this book on the usual websites, such as Amazon.

Please post your thoughts on Facebook or other networks that you use. Do not hold back in introducing your friends to this movement. You can join the CVM group on Facebook.

Together we could see many thousands of men becoming disciples of Jesus. We just need to spread the word.

Grace and peace.

XII